# FIRST STATS

NAME

BIRTHDAY

TIME OF BIRTH

BIRTHPLACE

WEIGHT

HEIGHT

# FIRSTS & FAVORITES
## a baby journal

created & illustrated by
Kate Pocrass

**CHRONICLE BOOKS**
SAN FRANCISCO

# FIRSTS

**FAVORITES**

# FIRSTS

# FIRST TIME I HELD YOU

# VISITORS PASS

WASH HANDS EXCESSIVELY (PARENTS ARE FREAKED OUT)

MUST SAY BABY IS CUTE (EVEN IF IT LOOKS LIKE AN OLD MAN)

MUST HOLD BABY SO THAT PARENTS CAN SLEEP

ADULT NOURISHMENT GREATLY APPRECIATED

# FIRST VISITORS

# FIRST HOME

NEIGHBORHOOD . . . . . . . . . . . . . . . . . . . . . . . . . . . . . . . . . . . . . . . . . . . . . . . . . . .

. . . . . . . . . . . . . . . . . . . . . . . . . . . . . . . . . . . . . . . . . . . . . . . . . . . . . . . . . . . . . . .

. . . . . . . . . . . . . . . . . . . . . . . . . . . . . . . . . . . . . . . . . . . . . . . . . . . . . . . . . . . . . . .

HOUSE . . . . . . . . . . . . . . . . . . . . . . . . . . . . . . . . . . . . . . . . . . . . . . . . . . . . . . . . . . .

. . . . . . . . . . . . . . . . . . . . . . . . . . . . . . . . . . . . . . . . . . . . . . . . . . . . . . . . . . . . . . .

. . . . . . . . . . . . . . . . . . . . . . . . . . . . . . . . . . . . . . . . . . . . . . . . . . . . . . . . . . . . . . .

ROOM . . . . . . . . . . . . . . . . . . . . . . . . . . . . . . . . . . . . . . . . . . . . . . . . . . . . . . . . . . . .

. . . . . . . . . . . . . . . . . . . . . . . . . . . . . . . . . . . . . . . . . . . . . . . . . . . . . . . . . . . . . . .

. . . . . . . . . . . . . . . . . . . . . . . . . . . . . . . . . . . . . . . . . . . . . . . . . . . . . . . . . . . . . . .

# FIRST BATH

# FIRST TIME OUT ON THE TOWN

- ☐ STROLLER
- ☐ CARRIER
- ☐ CAR
- ☐ BIKE
- ☐ ARMS
- ☐ _____

| HELLO MY NAME IS | HELLO MY NAME IS |
|---|---|
| CREATURE | SHORT STACK |
| HELLO MY NAME IS | HELLO MY NAME IS |
| LIL' PIE | HOBBIT |
| HELLO MY NAME IS | HELLO MY NAME IS |
| NUGGET | WIGGLE WORM |

# FIRST NICKNAME

# FIRST TIME YOUR EYES FOCUSED ON ME

# FIRST COMFORT ITEM

☐ PACIFIER
☐ STUFFIE
☐ BLANKIE
☐ _____

# FIRST TIME YOU SLEPT THROUGH THE NIGHT

# FIRST SMILE

# FIRST GIGGLE

TEE HEE

# FIRST TIME WE PLAYED PEEKABOO

# FIRST TIME YOU WAVED

PSYCHIC PARENTS NETWORK

# FIRST TIME I KNEW WHAT YOU WERE TRYING TO SAY

# FIRST WORDS

......................................................................................

......................................................................................

......................................................................................

......................................................................................

# FIRST TIME YOU SAID "NO"

......................................................................................

......................................................................................

......................................................................................

......................................................................................

# FIRST FOOD YOU WANTED MORE OF

........................................................

........................................................

........................................................

........................................................

# FIRST FOOD YOU DIDN'T LIKE

........................................................

........................................................

........................................................

........................................................

# FIRST TIME EATING SOMETHING SOUR

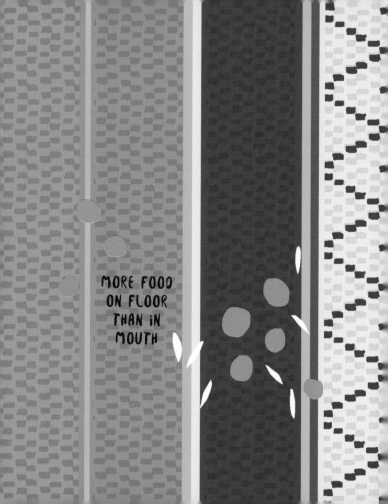

# FIRST TIME YOU FED YOURSELF

ALL IS FAIR IN
LOVE AND BABIES

TRIED TO WARN THEM

I'M MORTIFIED

IT'S THEIR FAULT FOR
REFUSING THE BURP CLOTH

EPIC LAUGHTER

# FIRST TIME YOU SPAT UP ON ONE OF OUR FRIENDS

......................................................................

......................................................................

......................................................................

......................................................................

......................................................................

......................................................................

......................................................................

......................................................................

......................................................................

BIOHAZARD

# FIRST DIAPER BLOWOUT

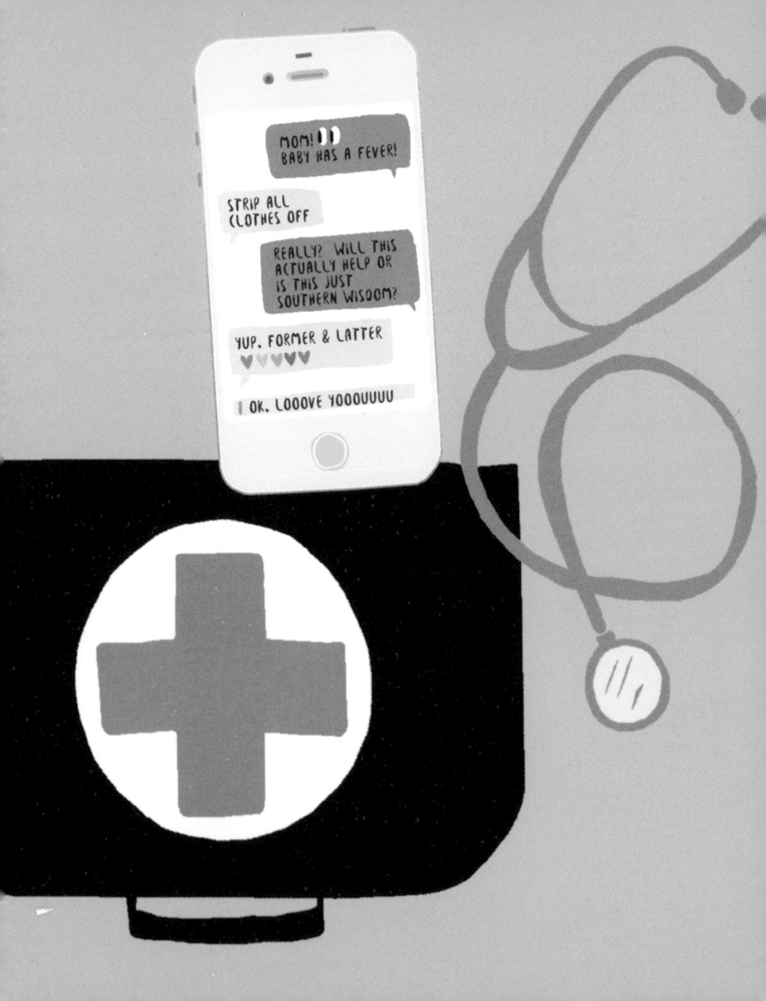
MOM!
BABY HAS A FEVER!
STRIP ALL CLOTHES OFF
REALLY? WILL THIS ACTUALLY HELP OR IS THIS JUST SOUTHERN WISDOM?
YUP. FORMER & LATTER
OK. LOOOVE YOOOUUUU

# FIRST FEVER

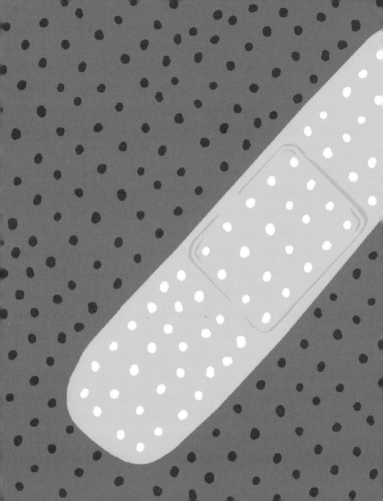

# FIRST OWIE

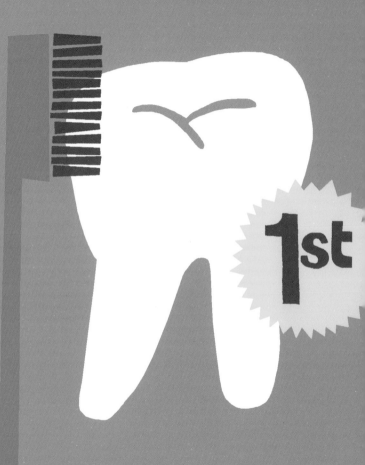

# FIRST TOOTH

# FIRST SCARE

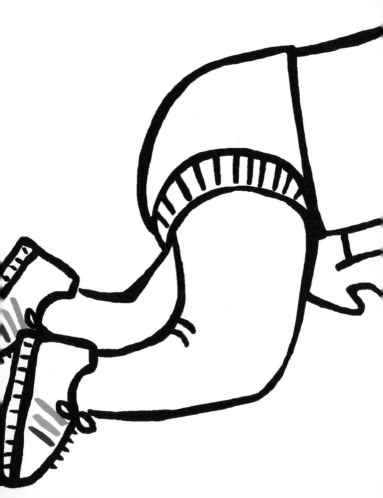

# FIRST CRAWL

# NOTICE

STRONG-WILLED BABY
ON THE MOVE
UNAUTHORIZED PERSONNEL
*-KEEP CLEAR-*

# FIRST STEPS

LOOK LIKE YOU'VE BEEN ELECTROCUTED

BABY MULLET

THICK LIKE A HEDGEHOG

BATH MOHAWK

ALFALFA

CUE BALL

PIGTAIL

# FIRST HAIRCUT

## FIRST HAIRDO

# FIRST TANTRUM

........................................................................

........................................................................

........................................................................

........................................................................

........................................................................

........................................................................

........................................................................

........................................................................

........................................................................

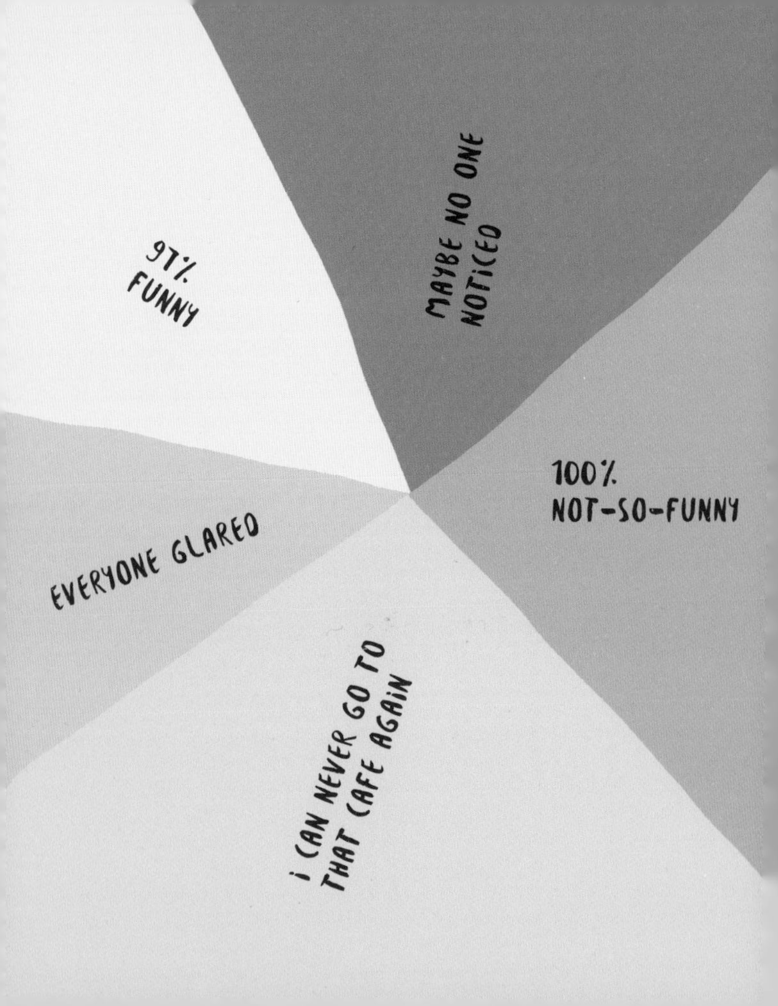
97%
FUNNY
MAYBE NO ONE
NOTICED
100%
NOT-SO-FUNNY
EVERYONE GLARED
I CAN NEVER GO TO
THAT CAFE AGAIN

# FIRST PUBLIC OUTBURST

# FIRST THING YOU DREW ON THAT YOU WEREN'T SUPPOSED TO

# FIRST REACTION TO WIND IN YOUR FACE

# FIRST TIME HOLDING A FLOWER

# FIRST NAP OUTSIDE

# FIRST ANIMAL INTERACTION

# FIRST TIME WATCHING A BIRD

# FIRST TIME YOU SAW A RAINBOW

# FIRST TIME YOU NOTICED THE MOON

# FIRST TIME IN AN OCEAN, LAKE, OR RIVER

# FIRST TIME WE WITNESSED YOU IN AWE OF THE WORLD

# FIRST VACATION

# FIRST TIME IN A BIG CITY

☐ ANTIANXIETY PLAN

☐ PACIFIER

☐ ZIPLOCKS FOR BLOWOUTS

☐ EARPLUGS FOR FELLOW PASSENGERS

IF FOUND
PLEASE
RETURN
TO

GRAN

(PARENTS NEED REST)

# FIRST FLIGHT

# FIRST RIDE ON A . . .

BUS .................................................................

....................................................................

BOAT ...............................................................

....................................................................

TRAIN .............................................................

....................................................................

BIKE ..............................................................

....................................................................

# FIRST PARTY WE TOOK YOU TO

............................................................................................................

............................................................................................................

............................................................................................................

............................................................................................................

............................................................................................................

............................................................................................................

............................................................................................................

............................................................................................................

............................................................................................................

# FIRST HOLIDAY

# FIRST COSTUME

# FIRST TIME DANCING

# FIRST BIRTHDAY AND HOW WE CELEBRATED

............................................................

............................................................

............................................................

............................................................

............................................................

............................................................

## ATTENDEES  ...............................................

............................................................

............................................................

# FIRSTS WE DON'T WANT TO FORGET

YOUR FIRST _____

YOUR FIRST _____

YOUR FIRST _____

YOUR FIRST _____

YOUR FIRST _____

YOUR FIRST _____

YOUR FIRST _____

YOUR FIRST _____

YOUR FIRST _____

# FAVORITES

☐ 1 AM WiDE AWAKE
☐ 6 AM CUTEST THiNG E
☐ 6 PM POSSESSED
☐ 9 PM BLiSSFULLY SLE

# FAVORITE TIME OF DAY

# WITCHING HOUR

| | | |
|---|---|---|
| ONLY FACING OUT | CALMING FOOTBALL HOLD | LIFTED REALLY HIGH |
| CRADLE OR BUST | ON SOMEONE'S SHOULDERS | BURP POSE |
| GENTLE SWAY | VIGOROUS SWAY | CONSTANT BOUNCE |

# FAVORITE WAY TO BE HELD

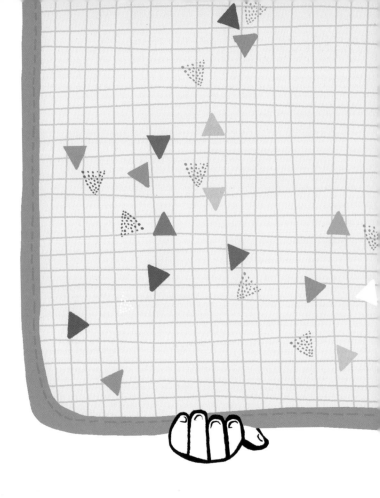

# FAVORITE THING TO CUDDLE WITH

WHILE GUZZLING MILK
CURLED UP WITH THUMB IN MOUTH
RIDING IN CAR
ARMS STRETCHED OVERHEAD LIKE ROCKY BALBOA
IN THE ARMS OF SOMEONE STANDING UNCOMFORTABLY
IN A CARRIER

# FAVORITE WAY TO FALL ASLEEP

ON THE FLOOR
WITH THE DOG

# FAVORITE PLACE TO TAKE A NAP

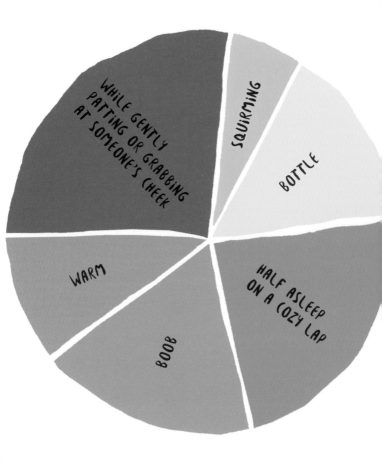

# FAVORITE WAY TO DRINK MILK

# FAVORITE FOOD TO ...

EAT ...................................................................

...................................................................

...................................................................

SPIT UP ...............................................................

...................................................................

...................................................................

THROW ................................................................

...................................................................

...................................................................

☐ SQUEEZE

☐ CHEW ON

☐ DROP

☐ THROW

# FAVORITE THING TO DO DURING A DIAPER CHANGE

# FAVORITE PERSON TO LAUGH WITH

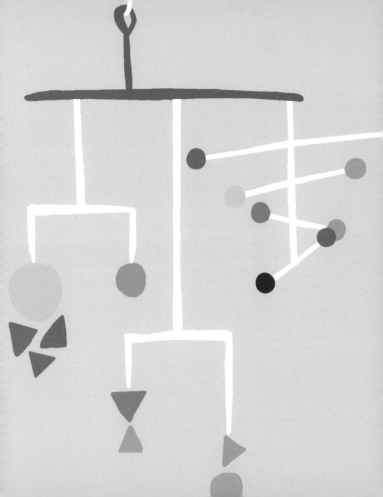

# FAVORITE THING TO STARE AT

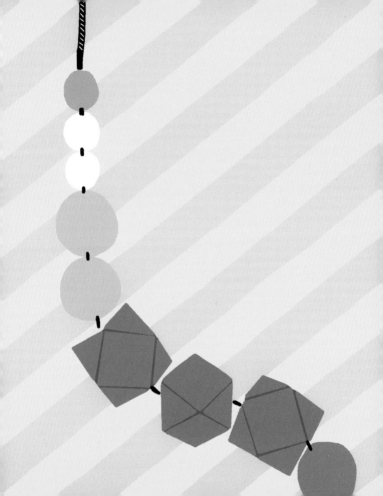

# FAVORITE ITEM TO GNAW ON

RAINBOW LIGHT
REFRACTIONS ON
THE WALL

# FAVORITE ITEM TO POINT AT

# FAVORITE ITEM TO GRAB

Weeeoo
oooooo
Weeeoo
oooooo
Weeeoo
oooooo

# FAVORITE NOISE TO BABBLE

# FAVORITE FACE TO MAKE

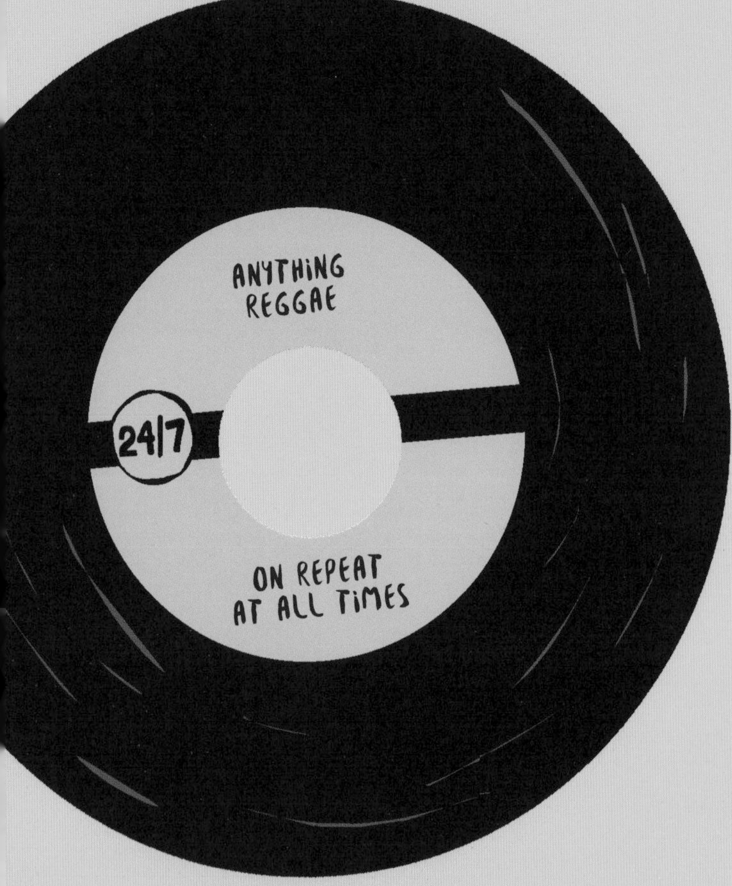
ANYTHING
REGGAE
24/7
ON REPEAT
AT ALL TIMES

# FAVORITE SONG

# FAVORITE BOOK

# FAVORITE CHARACTER

BLEAT

BLEAT

BAAAHHHH

# FAVORITE ANIMAL SOUND

# FAVORITE WAY TO MAKE A MESS

**DOG**

(NOT BABY)

# FAVORITE NAUGHTY THING TO KEEP TRYING

# FAVORITE BATH-TIME ACTIVITY

HEAD BOBBING TO
BLACK SABBATH

THAT THING YOU DO
WITH YOUR EYEBROWS

THE RIGHT FOOT CRAW
LEFT KNEE DRAG TECHNIQ

REACHING YOUR TOES
TO YOUR MOUTH

SHAKING OFF THE BATH
WATER LIKE A DOG

# FAVORITE TRICK TO SHOW OFF

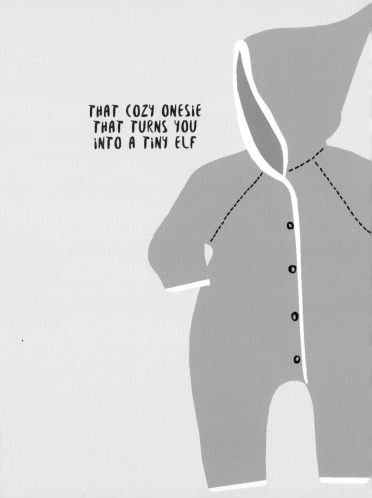

THAT COZY ONESIE
THAT TURNS YOU
INTO A TINY ELF

# FAVORITE CLOTHING TO WEAR

# FAVORITE WAY TO GET AROUND

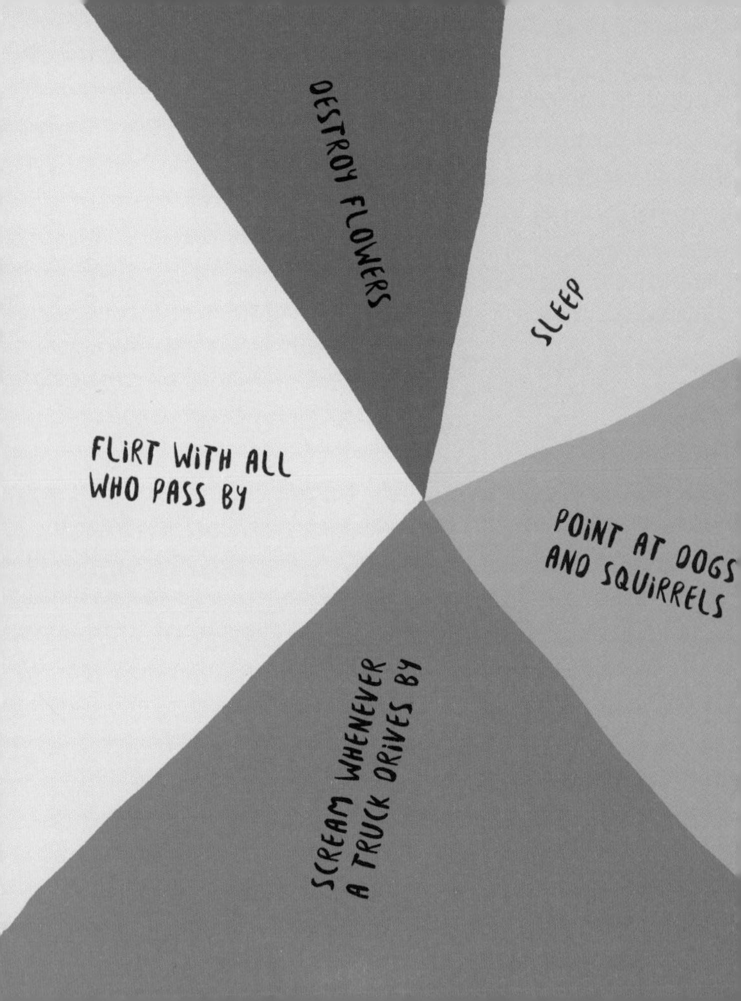
DESTROY FLOWERS
SLEEP
FLIRT WITH ALL WHO PASS BY
POINT AT DOGS AND SQUIRRELS
SCREAM WHENEVER A TRUCK DRIVES BY

# FAVORITE THING TO DO ON A WALK

# FAVORITE PLACE TO SIT

# FAVORITE OUTING

# FAVORITE THING TO DO AT THE PARK

# FAVORITE ACTIVITY

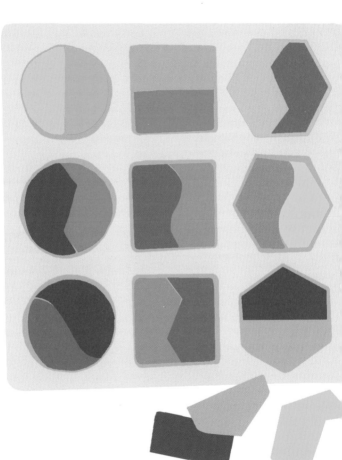

# FAVORITE GAME TO PLAY

DEEP IN TOE FASCINATION

# FAVORITE WAY TO ENTERTAIN YOURSELF

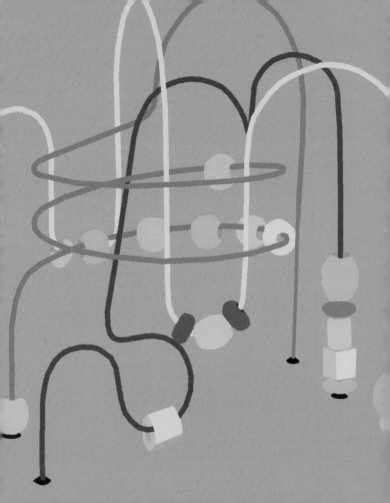

# FAVORITE TOY TO PLAY WITH

# FAVORITE TREAT

MURKY
LAKE

SMELL
THOSE
LILACS

ZIGGY
STARDUST
RED

FALL
MORNING
SUNSHINE

DIRT
ROAD

THE COLOR
OF YOUR
BLANKIE

BABY
POOP

SOOTHING
SKY

COSMIC
BLUE

# FAVORITE COLOR

NEVER
UNDERESTIMATE
THE POWER OF
THE BASHFUL
FLIRT

# FAVORITE WAY TO GET SOMEONE'S ATTENTION

NOWHERE ... NEVER
UNDER CHIN
ONLY BY GRAMMA
CROOK OF ELBOW
BELLY
BOTTOMS OF FEET
SIDE OF NECK

# FAVORITE PLACE TO BE TICKLED

# FAVORITE WORD TO SAY

# FAVORITES WE DON'T WANT TO FORGET

YOUR FAVORITE _____

· · · · · · · · · · · · · · · · · · · · · · · · · · · · · · · · · · · · · · · · · · ·

· · · · · · · · · · · · · · · · · · · · · · · · · · · · · · · · · · · · · · · · · · ·

· · · · · · · · · · · · · · · · · · · · · · · · · · · · · · · · · · · · · · · · · · ·

· · · · · · · · · · · · · · · · · · · · · · · · · · · · · · · · · · · · · · · · · · ·

· · · · · · · · · · · · · · · · · · · · · · · · · · · · · · · · · · · · · · · · · · ·

· · · · · · · · · · · · · · · · · · · · · · · · · · · · · · · · · · · · · · · · · · ·

· · · · · · · · · · · · · · · · · · · · · · · · · · · · · · · · · · · · · · · · · · ·

· · · · · · · · · · · · · · · · · · · · · · · · · · · · · · · · · · · · · · · · · · ·

· · · · · · · · · · · · · · · · · · · · · · · · · · · · · · · · · · · · · · · · · · ·

YOUR FAVORITE _____

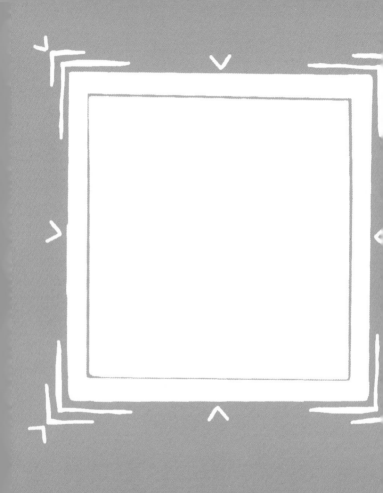

YOUR FAVORITE _____

YOUR FAVORITE _____

YOUR FAVORITE _____

YOUR FAVORITE _____

YOUR FAVORITE _____

YOUR FAVORITE _____

YOUR FAVORITE _____

ISBN 978-1-4521-6778-7

Manufactured in China

Designed by Kate Pocrass
See the full range of Kate Pocrass gift products at
www.chroniclebooks.com.

10 9 8 7 6 5 4 3 2 1

Chronicle Books LLC
680 Second Street
San Francisco, California 94107
www.chroniclebooks.com